CUTTING-EDGE TECHNOLOGY

ALL ABOUT APPS

by Christy Mihaly

FOCUS
READERS

WWW.NORTHSTAREDITIONS.COM

Produced for North Star Editions by Red Line Editorial.

Photographs ©: Georgejmclittle/Shutterstock Images, cover, 1; firemanYU/iStockphoto, 4–5; Rawpixel.com/Shutterstock Images, 7; Marripopins/Shutterstock Images, 9; hocus-focus/iStockphoto, 10–11; Stuart Monk/Shutterstock Images, 12–13; Burlingham/Shutterstock Images, 14; ymgerman/Shutterstock Images, 17; monkeybusinessimages/iStockphoto, 18–19; DragonImages/iStockphoto, 20; dennizn/Shutterstock Images, 23; Ole Spata/picture-alliance/dpa/AP Images, 24-25; Bart Everett/Shutterstock Images, 27; Matthew Corley/Shutterstock Images, 29

Content Consultant: M. Arcan Erturk, Postdoctoral Associate, University of Minnesota

ISBN
978-1-63517-010-8 (hardcover)
978-1-63517-066-5 (paperback)
978-1-63517-171-6 (ebook pdf)
978-1-63517-121-1 (hosted ebook)

Library of Congress Control Number: 2016949759

Printed in the United States of America
Mankato, MN
November, 2016

ABOUT THE AUTHOR

Christy Mihaly loves writing about science because it means she's always learning something new. She has written for young readers about topics including advanced solar power technology, genetics, and high-tech careers. She appreciates how apps help her work more efficiently and make more time for fun. Her publications include books, articles, stories, and poetry for readers of all ages.

TABLE OF CONTENTS

CHAPTER 1

APPS TO THE RESCUE

An overloaded truck bounces down a city street. It turns a corner too fast, spilling half its load onto the road. The driver speeds away, leaving a sour-smelling mess. A crowd gathers. Emergency workers arrive. What is that stinky stuff in the street? Is it dangerous?

Apps can help emergency crews determine whether substances are dangerous.

The emergency crew's captain pulls out her smartphone and gives it a few taps. Soon, she identifies the material. It's poison! The captain looks up how to clean the spill safely. She's using an app called Wireless Information System for Emergency Responders (WISER). WISER gives emergency workers the information they need to protect people. It's an app that saves lives.

You probably don't have a mystery mess on your hands. But apps can still come in handy. Apps can help you find a basketball score, listen to music, or get answers to homework questions.

Some apps help runners keep track of how far they have gone.

An app is a set of instructions that tells a computer or mobile device how to do something. Without these instructions, a smartphone would be a useless block of metal and plastic. The set of instructions that make a computer or device work is called **software**. It is written in **code**, a language that computers understand.

There are two kinds of software. One kind is the operating system. This runs the whole computer or device. The other kind is application software, which is also known as an app. Apps function within the device's operating system. Apps make a device do certain tasks, such as playing videos or translating words from one language to another.

Some apps turn a device into a tool, such as a flashlight. Many apps are games. Whether a person prefers solo brain games or online contests with many players, apps make these games happen.

Apps also keep friends connected. Apps let people chat by video, share

A flashlight app turns a smartphone into a useful tool.

photos, and send messages. Students
can even use apps for schoolwork. Apps
can track assignments. They make it
easy to do research and create charts or
slide shows. Apps can be useful in many
aspects of daily life.

HOW COMMON APPS CAN BE USED

Messages: texting

Photos: collect your pictures and videos

Calendar: keep track of dates and deadlines

Newsstand: newspapers, news videos, and more about current events

Contacts: list friends, family, and important information

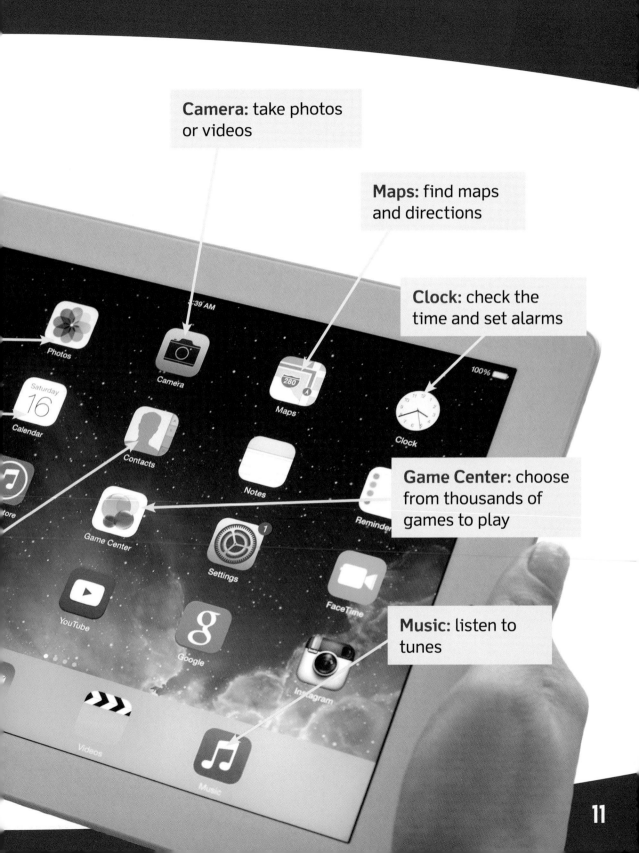

Camera: take photos or videos

Maps: find maps and directions

Clock: check the time and set alarms

Game Center: choose from thousands of games to play

Music: listen to tunes

CHAPTER 2

WHAT MAKES AN APP HAPPEN?

On a rainy day in India, 12-year-old Arjun Kumar was late getting home from school. Heavy rains slowed down his school bus. When Arjun finally arrived and saw how worried his parents were, he had a great idea. He wanted to create an app to let his parents track his school bus.

The Ez School Bus Locator app helps parents see where a school bus is.

13

 Apps can help doctors and nurses do their jobs more efficiently.

While still in seventh grade, Arjun developed the Ez School Bus Locator app. It allows parents to log on and check the location of their children's bus.

Many people create apps to solve problems. A problem is a chance to make things better. If a person wants to create an app but doesn't know how to write computer code, he or she might try using an app that teaches coding. Some programs even allow beginners to write apps without knowing code. For example, the Massachusetts Institute of Technology has an online tool called MIT App Inventor that makes app creation easy. Arjun Kumar used App Inventor for his school bus app.

When the Apple **app store** first opened in 2008, it offered approximately 500 apps. But that number quickly grew.

Other app stores started selling apps as well. Today's shoppers can choose from more than four million apps. Now there are hundreds of millions of downloads from app stores every year. And every day, more apps are being created.

SMILE FOR THE APP

People who can't see may not know when someone nearby is smiling. But an app called the Listerine Smile Detector can help them. This app uses a smartphone's camera to view people's faces. When the app recognizes a smile, it signals the user by vibrating the phone. This is one app that can really make people smile!

App stores usually show rankings so users can see how popular the app is.

CHAPTER 3

APPS ALL AROUND

Many apps are great for school. Other apps let people design construction projects such as bridges and towers. Some take users exploring around the world or through state capitals.

People can use apps to read or listen to books. Apps make it easy to search an ebook for certain words.

Some apps are games that help students learn math skills.

Cooking apps can be very helpful in the kitchen.

Users can also look up words they don't know. And by tapping a link in an ebook, users could play a video or visit a related website.

Apps can also be useful for researching and writing reports. Some apps steer users to reliable information sources. For the latest news from space, the National Aeronautics and Space Administration (NASA) has an app that provides articles, stories, photos, and videos. With a National Geographic app, people can see maps, facts, and statistics from all over the world. Still other apps help report writers when they are organizing their sources.

After school, apps continue providing facts, figures, and fun. Apps can provide weather forecasts, sports scores, and news. Health apps count how many steps a person takes each day and track the foods he or she eats.

Whether app users are looking for the nearest library, donut shop, or gym, a map app will point them in the right direction. Apps can tell people where to catch a bus. Messaging and video chat

WHAT TO WATCH OUT FOR

Before downloading a new app, there are two important questions to ask. First, users should ask if the app is safe. It's best to check with a parent or teacher to make sure. It's important to avoid apps that might let a virus into the system, fail to protect personal information, or cause other problems. Second, users should ask if free really means free. Sometimes a "free" app will ask users to pay for extra services. It's best to figure this out before downloading.

Map apps can be especially useful for finding directions in an unfamiliar city.

apps are also good for keeping in touch with friends and family. And of course, apps are great for games.

CHAPTER 4

APPS OF THE FUTURE

Apps of the future could solve many problems and bring on fresh fun. For example, some apps help people with disabilities get around on their own. For shoppers who can't read product packages, apps scan bar codes and read product information aloud.

Apps can help blind people determine when it is safe to cross the street.

Perhaps someday there will be apps that work by sensing a user's brain waves.

Apps that use global positioning system (**GPS**) technology know where a user is. Future apps will be able to provide details about what's happening at a user's location before he or she even asks.

Before getting home at night, a person could use an app to turn on the house lights from a block away. An app connected to a camera in a refrigerator could show users the inside of the fridge while they're shopping. Another app could turn on a person's favorite music when he or she enters a room.

Crowdsourcing apps can warn drivers so they don't get stuck in traffic.

Crowdsourcing apps collect and share input from many users. For example, some apps collect customers' reviews of businesses. People can report whether or not a restaurant serves tasty food, has rude waiters, or is easy to enter in a wheelchair. Crowdsourcing apps also let people share information not found in official news sources.

For example, during street protests, observers send reports to spread the word about what's happening.

With **virtual reality** apps, users can enter amazing 3D maps, models, movies, and more. **Augmented reality** apps show

GPS

The United States government runs the GPS system, which uses 24 satellites orbiting Earth. Smartphones and other mobile devices receive signals from these satellites, allowing device users to pinpoint their exact location on the planet. Apps that use this GPS system help people get where they're going. Apps help rescuers find lost hikers, help scientists track animals, and help farmers get information about their fields.

Games such as *Pokémon Go* use augmented reality.

users computer-generated images on top of real-world images. These technologies continue to improve, so they will likely become even more common in the future.

FOCUS ON
APPS

Write your answers on a separate piece of paper.

1. Write a letter to a friend explaining the main ideas of Chapter 4.

2. Do you think it's fair for app makers to charge for extra services on free apps? Why or why not?

3. What kind of app collects input from many users?

    A. sports
    B. weather
    C. crowdsourcing

4. Which app is most likely to use GPS?

    A. an app that gives new recipes to cook
    B. an app that shows a runner's route
    C. an app that helps with homework

Answer key on page 32.

GLOSSARY

app store
An online service people can use to find and download software programs.

augmented reality
Technology that adds computer-created images, graphics, or other information onto a user's view of the real world in real time.

code
Instructions that tell a computer or device what to do.

GPS
A navigation system that uses satellites to figure out location.

software
The programs that run on a computer and perform certain functions.

virtual reality
An artificial world that a person can interact with.

TO LEARN MORE

BOOKS

Beer, Paula, and Carl Simmons. *Hello, App Inventor!
Android Programming for Kids and the Rest of Us*. Shelter
Island, NY: Manning Publications, 2015.

Gifford, Clive. *Amazing Applications and Perfect Programs*.
New York: Crabtree Publishing Company, 2015.

Gregory, Josh. *Apps: From Concept to Consumer*. New
York: Children's Press, 2015.

NOTE TO EDUCATORS

Visit **www.focusreaders.com** to find lesson plans,
activities, links, and other resources related to this title.

INDEX

Answer Key: 1. Answers will vary; **2.** Answers will vary; **3.** C; **4.** B